WRITERS

ON

WRITERS

Published in partnership with

STATE LIBRARY VICTORIA
What's your story?

WRITERS
CERIDWEN
DOVEY
ON
J.M.
COETZEE
WRITERS

Black Inc.

Published by Black Inc.
in association with the University of Melbourne and State Library Victoria.

Black Inc., an imprint of Schwartz Publishing Pty Ltd
Level 1, 221 Drummond Street
Carlton Victoria 3053 Australia
enquiries@blackincbooks.com
www.blackincbooks.com

State Library Victoria
328 Swanston Street
Melbourne Victoria 3000 Australia
www.slv.vic.gov.au

The University of Melbourne
Parkville Victoria 3010 Australia
www.unimelb.edu.au

9781760640613 (hardback)
9781743820650 (ebook)

 A catalogue record for this
book is available from the
National Library of Australia

Cover and text design by Peter Long
Typesetting by Marilyn de Castro
Photograph of Ceridwen Dovey: Shannon Smith
Photograph of J.M. Coetzee: Ulla Montan

Printed in China by 1010 Printing

For T.J.M.D.

I was born in the year J.M. Coetzee published his third novel, *Waiting for the Barbarians*. My mother read this dark, disturbing novel with its many scenes of torture as she breastfed me at night, while my older sister slept and the house was quiet. It was 1980. The apartheid government had declared a state of emergency in the face of growing internal revolt, and my parents were thinking of leaving South Africa again.

My mother nursed me in the spare room so the lamplight wouldn't wake my father, and, as she read, her somatic response to the words on the page would have coursed through her into me: elation and despair, trepidation and longing. I feel I'm still marked by that embodied encounter with his writing, via my mother, as a newborn. Coetzee, who anticipates everything, would say I am inhabiting a fiction in imagining my way back to my neonate self, though even he allows for the possibility of flickerings of insight into other selves, or our own younger selves.

Several years later, when I was no longer a baby and my mother was on her way to becoming the first scholar to publish a book on Coetzee's work, I formed one of my earliest visual memories. It is of the striking cover of this same novel, which lay on the kitchen table in our Melbourne home, surrounded by the detritus of a midday meal: half-eaten sandwiches, apple cores. A picture of a white man on his knees, washing a pair of jagged black feet that have been sawn off at the ankles.

That image haunted me. I wanted to know what was inside the book that kept my mother in its thrall. I could sometimes pinpoint the moment when she fell through the trapdoor into the secret world of her mind, and I knew this book was one of the portals through which I might one day follow her there. She had taken over our dining room as her study, where she'd work from four until eight each morning, sitting on the floor in front of the heater in the chilly dawn hours, writing by hand in foolscap pads. When she came through to join us for breakfast, with rosy cheeks and bright eyes, I was aware that something special had happened to her in those hours, something to which I was not privy.

In Coetzee's 2003 novel *Elizabeth Costello*, the adult son, John, remembers that his mother 'secluded herself in the mornings to do her writing', while he and his sister would 'slump outside the locked door and make tiny whining sounds'. I felt no bitterness at having a door temporarily closed between my mother's world and mine, for there was never any doubt that my sister and I were front and centre of her life; her pleasure in the work of mothering was very evident to us throughout the long days we spent in her care. Instead, I was mesmerised by the way she could switch roles – effortlessly, it seemed to me then – and become immersed in these books written by a mysterious man whom she referred to only as 'J.M.'

Coetzee has always *been there*, an unseen but strongly felt presence in our small family drama. I suspect that it was at least in part owing to his presence that I first learned to take what psychoanalysts refer to as 'the third position' so crucial to a child's maturation, to let somebody else into the intense dyad of mother and child. The psychotherapist Arabella Kurtz, in the recently published correspondence between herself and Coetzee, explains this phase in the child's development as 'the ability to build a space in one's own mind for the relationships between others'.

Coetzee himself depicts this awareness in his fictionalised autobiographies *Boyhood* and *Youth*. The young John is very close to his mother – she is the firmest foundation in his life – but he senses with some unease that she has an interior life of her own, that she had 'a life before he came into being, a life in which there was no requirement upon her to give him the slightest thought'. The child has to grasp that the Other, usually in the form of the mother, has full personhood – and in so doing, the child intuits the scale of history, that almost unimaginable time, in the words of Roland Barthes, 'when my mother was alive before me'.

My mother came into the kitchen on those mornings – often clutching one or another of Coetzee's novels – in a heightened state of intellectual arousal, a state I have since come to know myself. Barthes vividly describes the *jouissance*, or bliss, that a 'writerly' text can produce in readers by encouraging them to expand beyond the usually passive subject position of the 'reader' and enter instead with the writer into a mutually satisfying interpretation of the text. In his fiction and critical commentary, Coetzee often describes the spark between writer and reader, master and student. He likes to portray teachers and students walking the dangerously blurred line between physical and intellectual attraction. In his correspondence with Kurtz, he mentions reading an interview with the actress Juliette Binoche, in which Binoche says she needs to have an erotic relationship with the directors of her films, or else the work suffers.

By this she doesn't mean she sleeps with them, Coetzee writes, but rather is describing the 'quintessential experience of learning, which is a feeling of growing beyond yourself, of leaving your old self behind and becoming a new, better self … a form of ecstasy'.

I'm now in my late thirties, the same age my mother was when she was in her most ecstatic phase of engagement with Coetzee's fiction. I've become acquainted, since having children, with the pace of domestic time, the way the mornings rush by and the afternoons pass as slowly as treacle. How the thought deprivation of early motherhood can be worse than the sleep deprivation, how sublime moments of reading and writing must be snatched in the day's natural lulls.

Like most people, I feel something akin to terror when I'm asked to respond to Coetzee's work, intimidated by the notion that his complex books are best parsed in the rarefied world of the academically ambitious. Yet my own most fulfilling experiences of discussing his writing have in fact taken place in more intimate settings. Once I was old enough to read his novels, the conversations I had about them happened over cups of tea with my mother and sister in the lounge room, or while we prepared dinner together, or during lazy mornings in our pyjamas on family holidays. I recently discussed *The Schooldays of Jesus* with my mother as she rocked my youngest son to sleep in her arms, and later skyped with my sister, Lindiwe (who is a scholar of African screen media in London), to talk about an article she co-wrote with our mother on film adaptations of Coetzee's novels a few years back. Her daughter was on her lap and every now and then we broke into a song to keep her entertained, to buy ourselves a few more minutes of conversation.

I feel grateful to Coetzee for introducing another dimension to our lives as women in the same family. We have each for decades been sustained by his work in different ways. And it strikes me as remarkable that Coetzee brought to life characters like Elizabeth Curren, Susan Barton, Elizabeth Costello, who are among the most intelligent women I've encountered on the page. They are mothers who are also thinkers. The one does not have to cancel out the other. The Elizabeths, in particular, pass on to their children not just an emotional legacy but an intellectual one, sharing with their offspring not only their bodies (wombs, breasts) but the contents of their minds.

The adult children in these books don't always respond well to their mothers' philosophising;

in fact, they are sometimes exasperated by it. Yet Coetzee is open to portraying the ideas that are transmitted between a woman and her children. These women characters have been criticised by some for not being believably *female*, or taken as mere stand-ins for the author, as if it's considered unrealistic for a woman to speak to her children about literature, philosophy, theory.

To me, these characters not only seem real but familiar: they remind me of my mother. Once I had embarked on my own life of the mind, in my late teens, she used Coetzee's novels to teach me how to think. Each one, she showed me, was a lesson in a different mode of knowing and method of representation; each revealed previously camouflaged codes of language. But the books themselves have remained fundamentally opaque to me. Even now, approaching him as writer *on* writer (a curious phrase that makes me imagine covering his body with my own), I can form no original opinion of his books that is not founded in my mother's way of thinking. To get to him, I must always step through her formidable mind.

Perhaps this is why I find myself regressing, whenever I read him, to an almost childlike state of wonder and bewilderment. I worship his novels but cannot interpret them without my mother's prompts, which in turn makes me feel helpless and resentful.

I was relieved to discover I'm not alone in this. In a 2012 essay, the South African scholar Hedley Twidle, who is around my age, admits there is something about Coetzee and his work that makes him behave strangely. He becomes childishly possessive, stalkerish, reluctant to teach Coetzee because he doesn't want to share him with anybody. He describes watching old footage of Coetzee in Cape Town and feeling certain that if he could only see Coetzee's bum clad in lycra as he heads off on one of his cycling routes, all of these confusing emotions would be resolved (in the footage, this wish is of course denied: Coetzee's jacket is too long).

To console himself, Twidle cites evidence in others of this same neurotic obsession with an author: Nicholson Baker over-identifies with John Updike, Geoff Dyer with D.H. Lawrence – and to these I might add Virginia Woolf saying of George Eliot that 'no one else has ever known her as I know her', or the novelistic portraits of mania-for-an-author created by Julian Barnes or A.S. Byatt. Twidle asks whether this 'obsessive-compulsive' response we have to the authors who mean everything to us can or should be tamed. He wonders what might happen if he let himself respond to Coetzee not with grave seriousness, but playfully, flippantly – if that, in turn, would allow Coetzee's books to remain fickle and wild.

My mother, like Twidle, has always been fiercely possessive of Coetzee's work. But she chose never to meet him, though there were ample opportunities to do so; she was satisfied to focus not on his biography – nor his lycra-clad body – but on his books. ('J.M.' – the initials are an act of distancing, a warning shot my mother heard clearly: do not come too close, you will not find me here.) Yet, to adopt Woolf's description of what a book can be, his novels seemed to issue a sly invitation to join in their 'dangerous and exciting game, which it takes two to play'. My mother felt invigorated reading him, but also baffled. What did Coetzee want from his readers and critics? For them to back off, or to come closer?

Encountering his work mimics that most primal encounter, in psychoanalytic terms, with the breast, which elicits the infant's rage and desire simultaneously. Coetzee writes in his fictionalised memoirs that John's first memory is of his mother's white breasts, and of feeling angry and confused that they had been taken away from him. The breast is offered, but then, inevitably, withheld. It is both wonderful and terrible, an object of the child's most powerful and conflicting emotions, which Arabella Kurtz describes as 'frustration, disappointment and longing, alongside feelings of love, calm and satisfaction'.

In a broader discussion with Kurtz about how people often fail to integrate two conflicting interpretations of past events, Coetzee interjects:

All that I see at the moment is the infant and the breast. The breast is good, the breast is bad: two conflicting judgments. How can it (it?) be both good and bad at the same time? What is the truth about it?

Our first lesson in life is to come to terms with this ambivalence. Perhaps the point of Coetzee's work – so much of which is steeped in his own deep readings of psychoanalytic theory – is to force us to sit with our conflicting judgements, to accept that his novels will never fully surrender their meaning. He refuses to answer our questions about them except, like Socrates, with more questions.

Reading his books can feel like a form of transference, whereby we unconsciously redirect feelings from formative relationships onto the figure of the author. By returning us to this childlike, childish state, maybe Coetzee is asking us to learn, as we did as infants, how to manage uncertainty, how to live with complexity: the project of a lifetime.

I'm holding in my hands my mother's copy of *Dusklands*, Coetzee's very first novel. It's the original Ravan Press edition from 1974. The paper jacket is torn at the spine, attached to the book by its folds alone.

The cover image is a watercolour of a South African landscape attributed to Thomas Baines – rocky outcrops, arid land, a few naked black figures and what look to be two clothed white ones. This is the frontier landscape which Jacobus Coetzee, J.M.'s ancestor and the narrator of the second half of the book, travels through in 1760, 'wreak[ing] vengeance on his Hottentot captors for daring to see him as a man, fallible and absurd, rather than as a white god', as the blurb copy puts it.

Coetzee's star burns so brightly in the firmament now that it's hard to imagine him in the role of debut author. It's as if he leapt, fully formed, from wherever it is that prodigies are made and took his rightful place among the literary greats. So I'm taken aback by the hedging tone of the description on the book's first-edition dust jacket: 'It is probably the first truly major modern South African novel and must be judged by the standards of the best modern fiction, with no qualifications whatever.' *Probably! With no qualifications whatever!* And the author bio on the now age-spotted back flap (no accompanying photo) is rather bizarre:

J.M. Coetzee was born in Cape Town in 1940. After ten years in Britain and the USA as student, lecturer, and employee of multi-national corporations, he returned to South Africa in 1971. He is presently a lecturer at the University of Cape Town. *Dusklands* is his first work of fiction. Among his interests are 'crowd sports; other people's ailments; apes and humanoid machines; images, particularly photographs, and their power over the human heart; and the politics of assent.' For the rest, he is 'one of the 10 000 Coetzees, and what is there to be said about them except that Jacobus Coetzee begat them all?'

It is a mind-warp to think of Coetzee as a mere *employee of multi-national corporations* and a lowly *lecturer*. And *other people's ailments* – what a thing to be interested in! Coetzee is a common Afrikaans surname in South Africa, which goes some way to explaining his final comment, but what author has the guts to put something this cryptic and confrontational on his first book? Why had I not thought of saying in my earliest author bio that among my interests are *apes and humanoid machines*?

In fact, as I learned from J.C. Kannemeyer's 2012 biography, Coetzee had not agreed to this bio – he later complained that it had been lifted without permission from a letter he'd sent to Ravan's publisher. What a pity it was not his idea after all. Yet it is intriguing to see an author who would later exert such strict control over the presentation of his books as a powerless first-timer. He disliked the insipid cover image too; he had suggested a black-and-white photographic plate from 1904, showing Khoisan people (the Indigenous inhabitants of the Cape) from the front and side, reduced to objects of scientific scrutiny. On that matter he'd similarly been overruled.

My mother's copies of Coetzee's first books

have the aura of relics for me because they reverberate with her passionate readings of them. As artifacts created just as he started out on his life as a published author, they also say something unexpected about who he was then, and can be experienced outside of all the padding and praise in which the later ones are swaddled. They are still trying to make their way in an indifferent world. Coetzee worked in relative obscurity for a while (publishers in London and New York turned down *Dusklands*), and even once he had become known within South Africa, he was not an international name for another decade or so. Part of the intensity of my mother's attachment to his work must have been linked to her sense of having stumbled on something and seen its worth before most others.

She ordered this copy of *Dusklands* in 1978, while heavily pregnant with my older sister, after seeing a flyer offering three new South African books for nine rand (then the equivalent of $9). Ravan was a new publishing house, and one of the few that was prepared to make minimal profits and face the risk of being shut down altogether in the prevailing climate of censorship in South Africa. She and my father were living in Pietermaritzburg, a small university town then dubbed 'sleepy hollow', where my father had recently taken a lecturing job.

My mother had grown up in this town and found it disconcerting to be back there. A dozen years before, she'd left to study physiotherapy at the University of Cape Town, and, after marrying young, she and my father moved to France, where he played rugby for one of the Bordeaux clubs. By day my mother worked as a physiotherapist at a clinic owned by rugby bosses; by night she studied for a distance degree, majoring in English and French literature. The reading lists for the courses never strayed from the official canon, and the lecture notes (which arrived in the mail) encouraged students to treat fiction in a F.R. Leavis kind of way – as a source of moral enlightenment and cultural continuity, almost an alternative to religion. Literary theory was anathema. The irony – of which she was then unaware – was that in Paris, only a few hours away by fast train, French theory was in its heyday.

Some years later she and my father had moved to the United States, where they both studied at the University of Oregon – not exactly the pre-eminent place for graduate studies in English literature, but my father was doing his degree in counselling psychology, and the department there had a good reputation.

In a memorable class taught by the critic Mas'ud Zavarzadeh, my mother encountered the shiny new term *postmodernism*, and read the metafictional works of American authors John Barth, Robert Coover and Donald Barthelme. She was fascinated by the reflexivity of their writing, by the way it was prepared to expose – even feed off – its own mechanisms, laying bare the way fictional selves are constructed. These revelations were deepened when she read Peter L. Berger and Thomas Luckmann's now-classic text on the sociology of knowledge, *The Social Construction of Reality*, published only a decade before.

But once back in Pietermaritzburg, she struggled to figure out what to do with these newfound ways of seeing the world. There didn't appear to be any way of reconciling them with the disquieting everyday realities of apartheid South Africa.

Soon after my sister was born, *Dusklands* arrived in the mailbox. My mother was stunned to discover a South African author who was writing reflexively, not just for the sake of cleverness or theoretical sophistication (as she felt many of the American authors were), but to draw attention to what it meant to write fiction from a compromised position as a white South African. It was a thrilling transgression, a political act in itself, for her to read a book so critical of the enterprise of empire – whether in the form of America trying to destroy Vietnam, or colonisers savaging the new world.

While she read, she felt as though Coetzee were writing just for her, in uncanny recognition of their shared history, both immediate and ancestral. From the scraps she gathered, she guessed that, like her, Coetzee was an English-speaking child of an Afrikaans father, whose forebears had been in the country almost from the beginning of European settlement. He too had been a student in Cape Town, then lived a peripatetic life, working and studying in Europe and the United States, before returning to South Africa.

She read *Dusklands* again. And again. Though she didn't yet know it, Coetzee was no stranger to that same *coup de foudre*. In *Youth*, there is a description of John buying a copy of Samuel Beckett's novel *Watt* from a second-hand bookstore, attracted by its violet cover and the notoriety of its publisher (Olympia Press published pornography as well as avant-garde fiction). 'From the first page he knows he has hit on something. Propped up in bed with light pouring through the window, he reads and reads.' John obsessively returns to Beckett's middle-period novels, from *Watt* to *The Unnamable*, letting this close reading influence the cadences of his own writing, and even his 'habits of thinking'. After discovering that the University of Texas at

Austin held Beckett's manuscripts (in the same archives that now hold his), Coetzee wrote his PhD thesis on Beckett, and was able to pore over drafts of *Watt*, set down in exercise books filled with sketches and margin notes.

When I recently reread *Dusklands*, I was assailed by the brutality of the imagery, the terrible scenes of rape and murder, of disembowelment. I found it hard to read the section in which Eugene Dawn stabs his young son with a fruit knife, or the passage where a pretty Hottentot child is shot between the shoulder-blades and hurled to the ground 'with the force of a horse's kick'. I asked my mother how she could possibly have read this with my sister at her breast. She responded that she was so stimulated by the intellectual challenge of his writing, so preoccupied by the mental activity of interpretation, that she scarcely registered the violence.

There is evidence of this in the marginalia of her copy of the book. In her handwriting, more familiar to me than my own, are snippets that let me peek inside that most elusive of places, parental consciousness. They are palimpsests of her readings over time, as she returned to the book over a period of years.

She notes themes as they emerge – *conventions of writing, evacuation, ingestion, totem and taboo* – and images that recur in both the American and South African sections: *livers, massacres, masters, penetration.* She underscores a phrase from the novel: *I grew out of books.*

These glimpses, while tantalising, are fragmentary. Why, for example, did she underline *he is now a failed creative person who lives vicariously off true creative people* on the first page of the novel? Why has she circled the word *fish* in the phrase *Gray planes, the shadowless green*

*light under which like a pale stunned deep-sea fish
I float ...?*

Once she'd finished reading *Dusklands*, my
mother went straight to the library to take out
In the Heart of the Country, which had been published in 1977. Then she waited impatiently
for another book by him, until finally, in 1980,
Waiting for the Barbarians appeared. In each
instance she began reading in a state of anxious
anticipation: what insights and understandings
would Coetzee give her? Would the new book
support the picture she was beginning to paint
of the greater project of his work, her hunch that
each of his novels was a meditation on different
modes of writing in the South African context?

When I look at the cover of her copy of *Barbarians* now, I feel a wave of nausea, something to
do with the vertigo of inhabiting my childhood
consciousness again. I have yet another memory,

from about the age of ten, of furtively paging through this book. The language frightened me. *One eye is rolled back, the other eye-socket is a bloody hole.* The sex scenes bewildered me. *There are moments – I feel the onset of one now – when the desire I feel for her, usually so obscure, flickers into a shape I can recognize.* I was horrified to find in the final pages a scene where the Magistrate has sex with a woman ('prostitute' was not yet in my vocabulary) while her baby sleeps in the corner of the room.

On the front cover – something I'd never noticed before – there is a glowing endorsement from Nadine Gordimer, who was then more esteemed than Coetzee (as colleagues they would have a complicated relationship for decades afterwards, especially after Gordimer, the champion of social realism and 'committed' literature, panned a later novel of his for 'lacking in political courage'). It is somehow heartening that even Coetzee's publishers once needed to ask his more illustrious peers for jacket blurbs with which to woo readers.

Coetzee's bio had by this stage been whittled down into a dry, impersonal form, but he must have given in to the demand to include an author photograph, for there is a small black-and-white portrait of him on the back cover. He has dark hair, a high forehead and jutting cheekbones, and a black beard – but half his face is in shadow, and he is looking past the lens. 'No photograph will ever tell the truth', he wrote in a later essay on Beckett, describing photographs in which Beckett was 'as lean as Kafka' and with the same 'piercing gaze', 'a man whose inner being shines like a cold star through the fleshly envelope'. He could have been describing himself.

When my mother first read *Waiting for the Barbarians*, the character of the Magistrate – the chief administrator of an unnamed frontier settlement supposedly threatened by barbarian hordes – made her think of her own male ancestors. Her father had been a provincial secretary, a bureaucrat from a long line of bureaucrats, the first of whom had been the magistrate of the hamlet of Swellendam in the Cape during the eighteenth century. Her grandfather had been the magistrate of a town in the Orange Free State while it was occupied by the British during the Second Boer War. An educated man who penned Latin inscriptions on the backs of family photographs, he was enlisted as a translator by the British officers because of his excellent English and bridge-playing skills.

My mother's father was gentle, contemplative. In his spare time he wrote poetry and painted small landscapes in watercolour. He kept *The Glory That Was Greece* and *The Grandeur That Was Rome* on his bookshelf. She could imagine him puzzling over the ruins and texts of ancient civilisations, as the Magistrate in *Barbarians* does. Cultured Afrikaners like her father did not want to be aligned with the Boers – uneducated Afrikaners whom they abhorred for being coarse, illiterate, brutish – but neither were they ever fully accepted by the English. These were the distinct cultural worlds between which Coetzee seemed to be navigating.

Waiting for the Barbarians was also a political allegory about the South Africa in which she and he were living. In 1976, thousands of black students in Soweto had protested against being forced to use Afrikaans as the language of school instruction. At least 150 people (with estimates of up to 700) – among them a child of thirteen – were shot and killed by police during the uprising. Black anti-apartheid activists, such as Steve Biko, the leader of the Black Consciousness Movement, were being tortured and killed in police detention. In this novel, Coetzee confronted the moral dilemmas of depicting political violence. How could he describe the abuses committed in the torture chamber without vicariously participating in the torture itself – and thus inadvertently supporting the state's project of terrorising and oppressing its subjects? 'The true challenge,' he later wrote, 'is how not to play the game by the rules of the state, how to establish one's own authority, how to imagine torture and death on one's own terms.'

In her copy, my mother has underlined *Pain is truth; all else is subject to doubt* and *The knot loops in upon itself; I cannot find the end.*

Next to a passage about a prisoner dying by falling against a wall, she has written *Biko* (the apartheid state claimed Biko's death in 1977 had been caused by injuries sustained in a scuffle with his captors during which he knocked his head against a wall).

She notes *Conrad, Kafka* alongside the most explicit scene of torture, where the Colonel writes the word 'ENEMY' in charcoal on the naked backs of prisoners before the guards beat them until the words are washed away by sweat and blood. She'd recognised the antecedent to this scene as Kafka's story 'In the Penal Colony', in which the Officer describes to a witnessing Traveller the workings of a torture device to be used on the Condemned. The man is to lie on a bed of cotton wool while a machine etches deeper and deeper into his body the phrase 'Honour your superiors', squirting water onto him to wash away the blood, mutilating him for twelve hours until he dies. But in the story's twist it is the Officer who finally subjects himself to the machine's torture.

The Magistrate in *Waiting for the Barbarians* repeatedly tries to establish himself as an altogether different kind of man to the Colonel, even as he becomes obsessed with understanding from the inside – intimately colonising – a young barbarian girl's own private bodily suffering. 'I must assert my distance from Colonel Joll! I will not suffer for his crimes!' he cries. Yet he is forced to admit that in fact he and the Colonel form a kindred pair as interrogators, 'one harsh, one seductive'.

My mother, too, was preoccupied with the spreading taint of the mass violence committed by the apartheid state in the name of all whites. Where on the scales of passive wrongdoing or active resistance should she place herself? The Traveller in Kafka's story thinks to himself, as he prepares to witness the torture, that 'it is always questionable to intervene decisively in strange circumstances … people could say to him: You are a foreigner – keep quiet'. Coetzee's novels gave my mother a vocabulary for her own divided identity – allowed her to speak to herself from *outside* herself – by carefully staging these conflicts and contradictions.

By the time Coetzee's next novel, *Life & Times of Michael K,* appeared in 1983, my parents had moved with us to Melbourne. My father had been getting strange calls in Pietermaritzburg in the early hours of the morning – a man speaking Afrikaans, saying *we know you are agitating politically at the university, we know you have a young family* (years later he found out there'd been a government informer in his department).

They had only bits and pieces of work, but my father convinced my mother to apply to do her PhD in the English department at the University of Melbourne. She was unsure of herself in a new country, still working part-time as a physiotherapist, and had two children under the age of four. When she got cold feet, he drove her to the university and insisted she hand in her application.

She knew she wanted to work on Coetzee, but at that time he was virtually unknown in Australia. Worried that a thesis devoted solely to his work would not be enough, she came up with the topic 'Postmodernism in Postcolonial Contexts' – a mouthful, literally and figuratively. She hadn't yet come to grips with what those terms even meant.

Forced to expand her focus, for the first year of her degree she read and published articles on contemporary Australian novelists: Peter Mathers, David Ireland, Frank Moorhouse, Murray Bail. At the same time, she was reading loads of theory, initially as a nervous new student in the compulsory postgraduate seminar on literary theory. Without a grounding in philosophy, she found much of it incomprehensible.

The breakthrough came when she read Gayatri Chakravorty Spivak's introduction to and translation of Jacques Derrida's *Of Grammatology*, and Anika Lemaire's book on Jacques Lacan. These two women had somehow managed to clear a space for themselves at the high table of theory that was then dominated by male academics. My mother was in awe of their courage. Spivak, for example, was only twenty-five and an unknown scholar recently arrived in America from India when she proposed to a publisher in the late 1960s that she translate Derrida into English and write a book-length introduction to his work, despite neither English nor French being her first language.

Deconstruction, Spivak believed, was never intended to be a means to pull things apart. In a recent interview about her long career, she said that deconstruction is 'not just destruction. It's also construction. It's critical intimacy, not critical distance. So you actually speak from inside.' She tells the story of her teacher Paul de Man once saying to another critic, Fredric Jameson, 'Fred, you can only deconstruct what you love.' It was Derrida's take on deconstruction, Spivak says, that led her to become one of the founders of postcolonial studies, or at least, it was 'that part of deconstruction which said that you do not accuse what you are deconstructing. You enter it.'

These days, literary theory seems mostly to be thought of as either pretentious or passé, but in the early eighties, even in universities far from Paris or the east coast of America, it was causing a stir. Theory felt significant, subversive – and, thanks to Barthes, sexy: texts could be experienced as long, slow seductions. Literary criticism should, according to Barthes, let the critic's pleasure be *spoken* instead of concealed.

Around the same time, Coetzee had to fight for his right to teach literary theory at the University of Cape Town, where, under a particularly conservative head of department, the English lecturers were still required to follow Leavisite principles, emphasising 'great traditions' (that is, British traditions) and practical criticism (close analysis of texts to probe their 'moral' worth).

In rebellion, Coetzee taught theory anyway. One of the genre-blending assignments he set his students was to write a fragment of a work in which Robinson Crusoe, upon reaching shore after being shipwrecked, finds himself in the Houyhnhnm Land of Jonathan Swift's *Gulliver's Travels*. A literary deathmatch: Defoe vs Swift! A cannibalistic carnival! The point, I'm guessing, was to get his students to think about which authorial voice would manage to 'eat' or overpower the other, and what might thus be revealed about the different modes of writing in these classic texts. ('I read mostly the stuff that, crudely speaking, I can cannibalise,' Coetzee later said.)

In 1984, we moved temporarily back to South Africa. My father had taken a one-year position at Rhodes University in Grahamstown, a university town even smaller and more colonial than Pietermaritzburg. The region was referred to as 'the Border', reflecting the history of frontier wars fought there between the Xhosa people and the European settlers. Around 4000 English settlers had been given land in the region in 1820, partly to help defend the frontier, and a huge and costly monument to them had been built in 1974. The monument was a concrete fortress on a hill, with a view of the distant township where black people lived in poverty. An inscription etched into the floor of the vast atrium read: *That all may have, and have abundantly.*

This region is the setting for Coetzee's 1999 novel *Disgrace,* which dramatises an encounter between the humanities – English literature, in particular – and the new voices of post-apartheid South Africa that were, by the late 1990s, beginning to challenge the assumptions of intellectuals like the flawed protagonist, David Lurie. In the wake of his involvement in a sex scandal in Cape Town, Lurie goes to stay with his daughter, Lucy, on her farm near Grahamstown, where she is living out her progressive politics by becoming 'a frontier farmer of the new breed' (with disastrous personal consequences).

Back in 1984, however, the English department at Rhodes University still liked to think of itself as the stronghold of 'English in Africa' (a journal by this name is still published from there), the supposed voice of civilisation in a deep, dark continent.

Soon after arriving, my mother gave a seminar on Coetzee's novels as Lacanian allegories, and remembers the faces of the mostly male, all-white English faculty growing ever paler as she used the term 'postcolonial' – the dirtiest word they'd ever heard.

We were renting a high-ceilinged old house on campus, where she again claimed the dining room as her study. My father often brought my sister and me to work with him to give my mother time to write undisturbed, and at weekends he took us to stay in a cabin on the coast, where my sister and I ran wild. 'Mommy is doing her P.H.D.,' we would say to anyone who asked where she was, knowing only that these three letters meant she spent a lot of time with books. By then, she'd admitted to her supervisor in Melbourne, the poet Chris Wallace-Crabbe, that she wanted to work only on Coetzee. 'I've been wondering when you'd realise you need to drop the Aussies,' he replied.

It was during this period that her work on Coetzee took off, as she tested her earlier intuitions about his novels against the theory she'd been reading. She took note of the character Magda's description from *In the Heart of the Country* of herself as a hermit crab, skulking in one empty shell after another, a parasite feeding on the cooling entrails of its host, 'wondering whose tissues it will live off next'. The scuttling hermit crab, the cannibalism of parasite and host: could these, she wondered, be metaphors for the way Coetzee adopted, adapted, *inhabited* other discourses, both theoretical and novelistic?

Derrida allowed her to see that Coetzee was deconstructing earlier modes of white writing, inhabiting them to offer a critique from the inside, not presuming that he could stand outside those texts that had shaped him.

She felt exhilarated doing her detective work, figuring out which clues he'd left as decoys, and where he'd left his tracks uncovered. A key source for *In the Heart of the Country*, she realised, was a novel, *The Story of an African Farm*, published in England by South African author Olive Schreiner under a male pseudonym in 1883. The ur-text for white South African writing in English, it is set on a farm in the Karoo semidesert region, where Schreiner lived for a period – a brave choice of setting, for she'd first had to reject the overbearing British literary tradition in order to feel justified in writing about the African landscape around her. (After the publication of *Boyhood*, many years later, it became apparent that in creating *In the Heart of the Country*'s setting Coetzee, too, was drawing on his childhood experiences staying at the Karoo farm owned by his grandparents – a place to which he returns repeatedly in his writing.)

It was the romanticised pastoral narratives of white South African authors – first English and later Afrikaans – that he was critiquing in the novel, my mother believed. Those earlier narratives voiced a longing for a lost rural past before industrialisation and urbanisation, but were incapable of acknowledging that this idyll depended on the systematic abuse of black people as slaves and labourers.

Magda is the first of Coetzee's many female protagonists. While she may or may not be overtaken by madness – she harbours, and perhaps carries out, revenge fantasies of killing her father and stepmother, and eventually begins communicating with the 'sky gods' – Magda is articulate about the stifling domestic norms imposed on her as a woman. She poetically evokes pastoral time, and cloistered female time, describing 'the desolation of the hour of the siesta chiming in cool green high-ceilinged homes where the daughters of the colonies lie counting with their eyes shut'. Yet she is aware that while she suffers as the daughter of a domineering patriarch, she is also part of a class of white perpetrators who oppress and enslave their black servants.

In a later essay on South African farm novels, Coetzee writes that Olive Schreiner was 'anticolonial both in her assertion of the alienness of European culture in Africa and in her attribution of unnaturalness to the life of the farm'. But even Schreiner – who resisted one form of paternalism by claiming space for female characters in a farm-world dominated by men – hardly mentions black labourers in her novel. Magda, on the other hand, yearns (as so many of Coetzee's characters do) to connect with the black people alongside whom she lives – her servants Hendrik and Klein-Anna – and yet she is unable to imagine what that connection might look like except as reverse-domination and abandonment.

Applying the same forensic analysis to *Waiting for the Barbarians*, my mother saw that the figure of the Magistrate might represent the stance of white liberal humanist South African writers such as Alan Paton, Nadine Gordimer and André Brink in their early works. In *Barbarians*, Coetzee undercuts this tradition of writing with empathy about the plight of black people and with shame about white guilt: he reveals the blind spots and assumptions about self and other embedded in this confessional mode, no matter how well-meaning (or self-flagellating) the author may profess to be.

The Magistrate, for example, believes in the steadyingly progressive hand of the law, dislikes violence, can admit to an incapacitating sense of guilt – and by the end, he has switched allegiances and subjected himself to the same torture that is inflicted on the oppressed. Coetzee, however, points subtly to the troubling nature of any act of moral witness or public suffering on behalf of others: that it can also be a means of absolving one's guilt, just as the Magistrate massages oil into the barbarian girl's broken feet in an act of self-gratifying penance for his own sins.

While my mother was painstakingly joining these dots, she was working in complete isolation.

There was virtually no critical commentary on Coetzee's novels, and even less information about him as an author. It's difficult for me to fathom this, now that we can find out about anybody and everything in the blink of an eye. Yet she was flying blind.

David Attwell's 2015 biography – written with access to Coetzee's meticulously annotated early drafts held in the University of Texas at Austin archives – includes notes for an early novel that Coetzee eventually abandoned, titled *The Burning of the Books*. They reveal a writer still trying to figure out what kind of fiction does *not* work:

(1) Fiction without a subject. (2) Fiction whose sole subject is apathy toward the notion of a subject.

Finally, Coetzee alights on something that *will* work, at least for him:

> (4) The possibility of rewriting another novel ... or of making that rewriting into the subject of your own writing.

For some later critics, this method of 'rewriting' – the way Coetzee builds his own novels on the back of his critiques of wider discourses of fiction and theory – started to feel frustratingly predictable. In his 2012 essay, Hedley Twidle complains about Coetzee's trick of alluding in his fiction to the other texts, the secondary reading list, one might need to seek out to understand the novels themselves. '[I]t all comes as a total, all-too-teachable package,' Twidle writes, 'a whole literary-critical paraphernalia, which you then assemble together in class like a Lego set.'

But imagine the thrill if you were the first to assemble that Lego set, all alone, fitting each novel into its previously camouflaged theoretical and philosophical foundations, seeing if each piece clicked into place. When my mother realised that Coetzee's novels 'did theory' on themselves, it was an epiphany of the kind that scholars live for, an insight that – once shared – seems self-evident to everybody else forever after because of its obvious *rightness*.

I t was around then that my mother decided to write a letter to J.M. Coetzee, in the hope that he might confirm she was on the right track. Long before email existed, she sent him a polite handwritten note, addressing him as 'Professor Coetzee' and asking if he might answer a few questions over the telephone about whether he considered his work to be postmodern, or in conversation with other postcolonial authors.

He was, at the time, back at SUNY Buffalo in New York State, on a visiting lectureship. His reply arrived in the mail a few weeks later, postmarked 21 March 1984. It was to be her first taste of Coetzee's dry humour, his reluctance to engage beyond the medium of writing and his refusal to be ensnared in earnest correspondence.

Dear Ms Dovey,

So you are at Rhodes University, that great centre of Postmodern research, and I am in the United States.

Is there anything you want to ask that can't be handled by mail? I am not a great believer in talk.

Sincerely,
J.M. Coetzee

She writes back, in May, this time responding in the same vein – arch, ironic – with a joke about post-structuralism's rejection of the notion of a stable centre and Grahamstown's backwardness: 'So who needs great centres (centres ? ?) of research – I came to Grahamstown for the night life.'

Then, unable to disguise how grateful she'd

be if he'd throw a morsel or two her way, she asks a few questions, mainly about whether he considers any other South African writers to be 'postmodern'.

Coetzee replies promptly from Buffalo on 6 June 1984, on an aerogramme printed with a collage of America's Olympic athletes. He won't let himself be cornered into accepting her terminology:

> I am not sure that I know what the term Postmodern means. If it means writing that does not pretend it is not writing, then Cervantes and Sterne are Postmoderns, and the term becomes a bit vacuous.
>
> Is South Africa really post-colonial? I would imagine that Grahamstown is one of the last places to give one that impression. All I can say in response to

this question – somewhat tangentially – is that high English realism (Austen, G. Eliot, James) is associated, here and elsewhere, not unnaturally, with the social intricacies of middle-class English society (which formed its main subject matter), and that if you are trying to get away from the one, you may want to try to get away from the other.

My mother only writes back six months later, in December. In the space of those months, both she and Coetzee have made international moves yet again. She writes from Melbourne to him in Cape Town, where he has returned to his position at the university.

Perhaps that is the reason for the long gap – having to pack up and move our family overseas once more. And maybe she is too tired to care anymore about being cagey and caustic, for she reverts to directness in her letter, asking him for very specific information, such as the date and title of his PhD thesis on Beckett, a copy of his inaugural lecture at UCT, whether he might shed any light on the philosophical sources for certain passages from *In the Heart of the Country* (she has already identified some of them as Lacan, Hegel, Blake, possibly Kierke-gaard), and what he considers to be the 'major generic categories of South African prose writing from its inception to the present time' (by this she means literary forms, such as explorer narratives, farm novels and so on).

At the end, she lets her guard down, signing off with, 'I have very much enjoyed working on your writing.'

From Cape Town, on 29 January 1985, Coetzee responds. It seems at first that he has relented, because he has enclosed a list of his publications, major and minor, and he tells her how to get hold of his inaugural lecture at the University of Cape Town, 'Truth in Autobiography'. But still he refuses to answer her core questions:

> You ask about the sources of various parts of *In the Heart of the Country*. I wrote the book a long time ago and don't know where to begin looking for the notes. Besides, don't you think it is the job of researchers to do that kind of detective work?
>
> You ask about the generic categories of S.A. prose. I've never given the subject any thought. Aren't the genres the same everywhere: novel, short story, essay, etc.?

His claim not to know where to begin looking for his notes on *In the Heart of the Country* may have been disingenuous, for the contents of his archive reveal that almost every source, note and draft was documented, dated and stored in an orderly fashion. But my mother was encouraged by his characterisation of researchers as detectives, for this was precisely the methodical, riddle-solving approach she'd been applying to his work.

She managed to track down a copy of his inaugural lecture, printed as a pamphlet by the university. It has a pale blue cover, now browning, and within it are further barbs, questions that Coetzee poses but won't answer about the 'privilege of criticism' in thinking it can tell the truth of literature. The final line is a powerful challenge to his (future) critics: 'If the desire of literary criticism is to tell every truth, to unveil whatever is veiled, to expose very [sic] secret to sight, why does it not tell its own secrets? Or does it claim to have none?'

She never wrote to him again.

In 1988, she published the first book on his work, *The Novels of J.M. Coetzee: Lacanian Allegories*. The cover image is a watercolour of Coetzee's eyes and a hermit crab emerging – a bit creepily, *Silence of the Lambs*–style – from his mouth, against a violet background. The illustrator based it on my mother's own paintings of hermit crabs.

The book is long, and dense with passages of quoted theory. As an adult, I've tried often to read it, each time hoping that I might finally be worthy of understanding – and each time coming away defeated by its sharp-edged brilliance. My mother wryly says that it's unreadable, that she was badly served by her publisher and had no useful input from an editor to make it more accessible to non-specialist readers. She still feels affectionately about it, though, because it represents the journey she took all those years ago, following Coetzee's lead, into realms of theory and philosophy that she might never otherwise have encountered.

Holding her book in my hands sometimes saddens me. It is a material reminder that intellectual passion ebbs and flows; that women's careers are always vulnerable to being truncated, subsumed by family responsibilities; that daughters grow up and mothers grow old. It is the first book she wrote on his work, and it is also her last.

Coetzee's allergic reaction to any interlocutor who wants him to make the meaning of his work explicit is now well documented. He detests being interviewed, seeing it as an exchange with a 'complete stranger' who is 'permitted by the conventions of the genre to cross the boundaries of what is proper in conversation between strangers'. Interviewers, he thinks, use 'rapiers of surprise' to force 'a flow of speech'. More than that, critic/interviewer and creator are adversaries, engaged in a duel where somebody is always left bleeding to death at the end.

Despite knowing this, I have to admit I felt a bit stung on my mother's behalf when I first read Coetzee's replies to her letters. Was he treating her like a little girl trespassing on things she shouldn't, closing the door as she tried to find a way in? Or was he doing her a favour by inducting her into the school of humiliation, a rite of passage in any emerging scholar's life? In Kannemeyer's biography there's a story about Coetzee writing to Beckett's publisher in 1968 after completing his dissertation, asking for permission to quote from Beckett's first published work of fiction, a collection of interlinked stories, *More Pricks Than Kicks*. Responding via his publisher, Beckett laid down restrictive – even humiliating – terms for the young man who had just spent years writing a PhD on his work: 'You may give permission for ten extracts (maximum), no extract to exceed ten lines.'

When I finally shared with my mother my negative feelings about Coetzee's replies to her, she responded emphatically that she doesn't think of their correspondence in this way at all.

'He could have had no idea about my back-story, how recently I'd come to those terms,' she told me. 'And in fact I appreciated his refusal to be bound by terminology. Theory is always fleeting. It dates so quickly. I liked that he made me question the very framework I was using to engage with literature at the time. He was a hundred steps ahead of me, but he was a hundred steps ahead of *everyone* – so I couldn't take it personally.'

She has great respect for Coetzee's refusal to interpret his own work, regarding it as a matter of life and death for him: it keeps his ability to create alive, an ability that itself takes an enormous toll. 'Writing is a matter of giving and giving and giving, without much respite,' he has said. 'I think of the pelican that Shakespeare is so fond of, that tears open its breast in order to feed its offspring on its blood.' Elsewhere, he commends Jonathan Franzen's decision to stop giving promotional interviews for a time because 'the repetitions of a single account of his own life were scouring so deep a trace that he would soon lose his freedom to interpret (remember) his life otherwise'.

Over the years, the only form Coetzee has allowed himself to be drawn out in is correspondence entered into by choice, a more dialogic exchange than the interrogative violence of interviews. This started in 1992, with his published dialogues with Attwell (who had been his student and became an early scholar of Coetzee's work), and has continued, more recently, in his published correspondence with the novelist Paul Auster and with Arabella Kurtz. For Coetzee, this kind of exchange mimics the entry into psychotherapy, a process of 'seeking the right person to talk to'. Even in these interactions, however, he can be stern and contrarian, and he establishes strict boundaries (he also always has the last word). There is an occasional sadism to his responses, as if he is playing with his prey before killing it.

I felt better about how he'd responded to my mother's letters when I read his correspondence with Paul Auster. They write to each other as friends, but still Coetzee can't help putting Auster firmly in his place, even as Auster does backflips and somersaults, trying desperately to keep Coetzee interested. When Auster waxes lyrical about the aesthetic pleasures of watching sport, Coetzee writes, 'I am dubious about this approach, and for a number of reasons.' You can trust he names them all. Auster makes the mistake of confessing that he has been 'rather bored' by an edition of Beckett's letters. Coetzee doesn't deign to respond to this, and a couple of letters later, Auster ashamedly retracts his comment ('It is not boring. Far from it …').

At one point Coetzee emails Auster's wife, the writer Siri Hustvedt, asking if she can recommend 'a good book or article that I can read to get an idea of [Beckett's psychoanalyst] Bion's approach to therapy?' Of course she would never respond to *him* that a good researcher should do that kind of detective work for himself.

My mother, sensing I was still struggling to accept that she had been inspired, not demeaned, by his replies to her letters, reminded me that Coetzee himself, back in 1986, had written a novel composed of letters addressed by a woman with no real cultural power to a famous male author. In *Foe*, he'd staged this writer-on-writer genre rather graphically by having the marginal, would-be author, Susan, straddle the famous author, Foe, for what Foe afterwards calls 'a bracing ride'.

I decided I should probably read *Foe* again.

Foe tells the story of Susan Barton, who is sending letters to the famous author Daniel Foe (Defoe's real name), in the hope that he will write on her behalf an account of her time shipwrecked on a desert island with Cruso and Friday. The letters seem mostly to remain unread by Foe; one is even returned to her unopened. He never writes back directly.

In *Foe*, my mother believes, Coetzee was addressing the dilemmas of feminism at that moment in history: how do women find a speaking position for themselves, how do they erect a self outside the family, outside the colonies, outside the patriarchy? Can and should feminism align itself with postcolonialism, or does this let one form of freedom and empowerment cancel out the other?

Susan Barton, shipwrecked while searching for her abducted daughter, is paired with Friday, a black man who has been rendered mute by having his tongue cut out. When she is first cast ashore on the island where he is slave to Cruso, Friday carries Susan on his back, and she soon becomes Cruso's 'second subject'. She lets Cruso have sex with her in a single instance – almost as a bid to exclude Friday from their uncomfortable triangle – and on the ship returning to England after their rescue has to pretend to be his wife, thereafter going by the name Mrs Cruso.

In England, after tiring of writing and speaking 'into a void, day after day, without answer', Susan finally uses her body to gain access to the famous writer Foe. As they sleep together, he bites her lip and sucks on it, murmuring, 'This is my manner of preying on the living.'

The novel ends on a thin note of hope that Susan and Friday might mutually affirm 'the existence of a secret self on the frontier between language and silence', a self they keep hidden from men like Cruso and Foe. They face each other underwater, and from Friday comes something '[s]oft and cold, dark and unending', beating against Susan's eyelids.

My mother was right, I realised as I finished *Foe*: Coetzee *has* always been ahead of the pack, challenging the rest of us to keep up, resisting our attempts to pin him down. For it's at this frontier between language and silence that Coetzee's writing constantly tries to locate itself. Through his characters who exist at the fringes of society, he gestures towards a desire to creep over the border of what it's possible to utter, to test the limits of the sayable.

*S*o this is art, he thinks, and this is how it does *its work! How strange! How fascinating!* These lines from *Disgrace* stopped me in my tracks when I first read them, for this was exactly the feeling I'd had as my mother initiated me into new ways of reading fiction: that things on the page are not always what they seem, that meaning is never stable.

It had a powerful effect on me, to sense so young that there were mysteries both about her and about novels that could not be solved. Unless, perhaps, I could worm my way *inside* the creative process, experience it from the inside out, by becoming a writer – and one day a mother – myself. Maybe then I would finally understand.

When my first novel, *Blood Kin*, was almost

ready to be published in 2007, my American editor – without knowing anything of my mother's history with Coetzee's work – sent a proof copy to him in Adelaide. It was such a long shot that she didn't tell me, assuming she'd never hear back. A few weeks later, we were gobsmacked when he sent her a blurb quote that would take pride of place on the book's cover.

I immediately called to tell my mother in Sydney, where my parents had moved permanently in 1999, a few years before Coetzee moved to Adelaide.

'He must be thinking, these Dovey women just won't leave me alone!' I said to her, high on hubris.

'My darling,' she replied, ever humble, 'I doubt he's even made the connection.'

Years later, soon after the birth of my first child, Coetzee blurbed my second book,

Only the Animals. I knew by then that he endorses books by many younger authors – whether or not their mothers once wrote about his work. This is an act of true generosity: many famous authors refuse to give quotes, even if they themselves depended on them earlier in their careers. Coetzee's name on a book by an unknown author immediately imparts a gravity to whatever is between the pages. His kindness in being prepared to do this still humbles me.

My mother read a draft of my gushing email of thanks to him after the second blurb and said, 'You can't send this! I told you he never traffics in earnestness!'

But I sent it anyway. Like so many others, I tried to find a point of connection with him through his passion for cycling, and mailed him a book of photographs called *Cycling's Golden Age.* I contemplated sending cycling gloves too, but at the last moment baulked at knowing which size to get. Of course I didn't tell my mother about the gift; my email was bad enough.

One morning soon afterwards I found a short email from John Coetzee waiting in my inbox, thanking me for the book. I had to sit down – I'd gone weak at the knees.

When Coetzee was awarded the Nobel Prize in Literature in 2003, his moving acceptance speech surprised and delighted the audience in the Stockholm City Hall:

> '*Mommy, Mommy, I won a prize!*' … Why must our mothers be ninety-nine and long in the grave before we can come running home with the prize that will make up for all the trouble we have been to them?

A year after his mother's death in 1985, Coetzee began work on *Age of Iron*, one of the very few of his novels to include a dedication. In the space of working on it, Coetzee also lost his father (in 1988) and his son (in 1989), and the book is dedicated to all three family members.

Certain passages of the novel are difficult to read for being raw with the grief of loss – parents of children, children of parents. Coming home after being told by her doctor that she has cancer, Elizabeth Curren remembers waking her daughter as a child, her little body warm, her breath milky, and the embrace they shared, 'the secret meaning of which, the meaning never spoken, was that Mommy should not be sad, for she would not die but live on in you'.

While my mother interprets this image as an allegory of reading and writing, I was touched by the beautiful if bittersweet description of the bond between mother and child. This is the perplexing quality about Coetzee's books, something noted by many commentators: for all their abstruse intellectualism, they can, at times, be heartbreaking. So many of the protagonists, the critic Theo Tait has pointed out, 'berate themselves for being cold and passionless', yet they also seek connection and transcendence; they long to slip their chains and turn their faces to the light, as Coetzee once said of his creations.

In his recent Jesus novels, for example, Coetzee seems to be expressing a frustration that reason is an overemphasised human faculty, and hints at a wish that we could more often experience these instances of haptic grace – like the dance the boy David learns in *The Schooldays of Jesus*, which allows him to 'call the numbers down from the stars'. I think my mother might be one of the few readers to feel a kinship with this novel; most of the reviews were tepid or puzzled. For her, it holds particular interest because she read it as she was teaching my oldest son to read, when he was about the same age as David in *Schooldays*. Coetzee has written in his letters to Kurtz of children who, if they're lucky, learn to love reading as a mysterious and deeply empathic act of 'finding one's way into the voice that speaks from the page, the voice of the Other, and inhabiting that voice, so that you speak to yourself … from outside yourself'. There is something poignant for my mother about the way Coetzee, with no grandchildren of his own, is imagining grandfatherhood through the figure of Simón, the old man helping to raise David.

At the academy of dance where David is enrolled, the teachers encourage him to stay in touch with the universe's dance, which he can still faintly recollect from his life before birth but doesn't have the words to express. To call the numbers down from the stars, the children need to dance with body and soul. 'Words are feeble,' says Ana Magdalena, the teacher. 'That is why we dance.' Her husband, Señor Arroyo, is awed by how the children move effortlessly across the abyss separating reason from empathy, while adults 'stand paralysed, gazing on the gap that yawns between us and the stars'. (Coetzee is writing from experience here: in *Youth*, the dance lessons John takes as a university student are a failure because '[n]ever for a moment, even during the lessons, was he really giving himself to the dance … he remained rigid with resistance'.)

What the adults in *The Schooldays of Jesus* seem to envy most is the children's ability to be open to moments when something other than their conscious, rational mind is able to impinge on their thinking, their feeling. Coetzee writes to Kurtz that he believes there is something larger than the self, but 'I don't know that one can actually get there or stay there for long'. All we can hope for is an instant when 'the veil opens and one has a flash of insight'. This happens to Simón at the very end of the novel. After years of depending heavily on reason, he begins to learn to dance. 'Arms extended, eyes closed, he shuffles in a slow circle. Over the horizon the first star begins to rise.'

My mother gave up writing professionally on Coetzee for many reasons, some personal, some political, from lack of conviction but also lack of confidence. After reading *The Schooldays of Jesus*, she felt she had been right to stop trying to resolve things in Coetzee's work. She now thinks that applying theory to his novels, using reasoned critical discourse to dismantle and decode them, may have been fundamentally against the grain of what the novels themselves ask for.

She has come to believe that Coetzee should be left in peace. Like his character Magda, he should be allowed to remain an 'enigma with a full soul' rather than one 'emptied of . . . secrets'. His books might instead be accepted as invitations to dance, opportunities to recall for an instant, as the boy David does, and the old man Simón too, what it feels like to close the gap between self and stars.

BOOKS BY J.M. COETZEE

FICTIONALISED AUTOBIOGRAPHY

Boyhood: Scenes from Provincial Life (1997)

Youth: Scenes from Provincial Life II (2002)

Summertime (2009)

SHORT FICTION

The Lives of Animals (1999)

Three Stories (2014)

CORRESPONDENCE

Here and Now: Letters 2008–2011
(with Paul Auster, 2013)

*The Good Story: Exchanges on Truth, Fiction
and Psychotherapy* (with Arabella Kurtz, 2015)

ESSAYS

Truth in Autobiography (1984)

*White Writing: On the Culture of Letters
in South Africa* (1988)

Doubling the Point: Essays and Interviews
(edited by David Attwell, 1992)
Giving Offense: Essays on Censorship (1996)
The Novel in Africa (1999)
Stranger Shores: Literary Essays,
1986–1999 (2001)
Inner Workings: Literary Essays,
2000–2005 (2007)
Late Essays: 2006–2017 (2017)